S0-BDP-743

Being Gay, Staying Healthy

The Gallup's Guide to Modern Gay, Lesbian, & Transgender Lifestyle

Being Gay, Staying Healthy

by Jaime Seba

Mason Crest Publishers

MASON CREST PUBLISHERS INC.
370 Reed Road
Broomall, Pennsylvania 19008
(866)MCP-BOOK (toll free)
www.masoncrest.com

First Printing
9 8 7 6 5 4 3 2 1

Library of Congress Cataloging-in-Publication Data
Seba, Jaime.
  Being gay, staying healthy / by Jaime Seba.
      p. cm. — (The Gallup's guide to modern gay, lesbian, & transgender lifestyle)
  Includes bibliographical references and index.
  ISBN 978-1-4222-1744-3 (hardcover) — ISBN 978-1-4222-1758-0 (series)
  ISBN 978-1-4222-1864-8 (pbk.) — ISBN 978-1-4222-1863-1 (pbk. series)
  1. Homosexuality—Psychological aspects—Juvenile literature. 2. Gays—Psy-
chology—Juvenile literature. 3. Gays—Health and hygiene—Juvenile literature. 4.
Gays—Sexual behavior—Juvenile literature. 5. Lesbians—Psychology—Juvenile
literature. 6. Lesbians—Health and hygiene—Juvenile literature. 7. Lesbians—
Sexual behavior—Juvenile literature. I. Title.
  HQ76.26.S428 2011
  306.76'6—dc22
                              2010020670

Produced by Harding House Publishing Service, Inc.
www.hardinghousepages.com
Interior design by MK Bassett-Harvey.
Cover design by Torque Advertising + Design.
Printed in the USA by Bang Printing.

Contents

PICTURE CREDITS

a4Stockphotos, Fotolia: p. 27
AgenceDER, Fotolia: p. 41
Alien Cat, Fotolia: p. 15
Ambro, Fotolia: p. 12
Byron, Rob; Fotolia: p. 49
Centers for Disease Control and Prevention: p. 36
Chan, Kit Wai; Fotolia: p. 22
Crisharvey, Fotolia: p. 30
Damkier, Mikael; Fotolia: p. 53
Dixon, Todd; Fotolia: p. 47
Eléonore H., Fotolia: p. 55
Galaxy Photo, Fotolia: p. 25

Kaulitzki, Sebastien; Fotolia: p. 50
Kaveney, Wendy; Fotolia: p. 52
Kurhan, Fotolia: p. 42
MacX, Fotolia: p. 35
Monkey Business, Fotolia: p. 29
Pejalaya, Fotolia: p. 24
Rodriguez, Andres; Fotolia: p. 58
Sanyal, Fotolia: p. 56
Stitt, Jason; Fotolia: p. 13
Swede, Chrisinda; Creative Commons: p. 11
ZTS, Fotolia: p. 39
Young, Lisa F.; Fotolia: p. 17

Introduction

We are both individuals and community members. Our differences define individuality; our commonalities create a community. Some differences, like the ability to run swiftly or to speak confidently, can make an individual stand out in a way that is viewed as beneficial by a community, while the group may frown upon others. Some of those differences may be difficult to hide (like skin color or physical disability), while others can be hidden (like religious views or sexual orientation). Moreover, what some communities or cultures deem as desirable differences, like thinness, is a negative quality in other contemporary communities. This is certainly the case with sexual orientation and gender identity, as explained in *Homosexuality Around the World*, one of the volumes in this book series.

Often, there is a tension between the individual (individual rights) and the community (common good). This is easily visible in everyday matters like the right to own land versus the common good of building roads. These cases sometimes result in community controversy and often are adjudicated by the courts.

An even more basic right than property ownership, however, is one's gender and sexuality. Does the right of gender expression trump the concerns and fears of a community or a family or a school? *Feeling Wrong in Your Own Body*, as the author of that volume suggests, means confronting, in the most personal way, the tension between individuality and community. And, while a community, family, and school have the right (and obligation) to protect its children, does the notion of property rights extend to controlling young adults' choice as to how they express themselves in terms of gender or sexuality?

Changes in how a community (or a majority of the community) thinks about an individual right or responsibility often precedes changes in the law enacted by legislatures or decided by courts. And for these changes to occur, individuals (sometimes working in small groups) often defied popular opinion, political pressure, or religious beliefs. Some of these trends are discussed in *A New Generation of Homosexuality*. Every generation (including yours!) stands on the accomplishments of our ancestors and in *Gay and Lesbian Role Models* you'll be reading about some of them.

One of the most pernicious aspects of discrimination on the basis of sexual orientation is that "homosexuality" is a stigma that can be hidden (see the volume about *Homophobia*). While some of my generation (I was your age in the early 1960s) think that life is so much easier being "queer" in the age of the Internet, Gay-Straight Alliances, and Ellen, in reality, being different in areas where difference matters is *always* difficult. Coming Out, as described in the volume of the same title, is always challenging—for both those who choose to come out and for the friends and family they trust with what was once a hidden truth. Being healthy means being honest—at least to yourself. Having supportive friends and family is most important, as explained in *Being Gay, Staying Healthy.*

Sometimes we create our own "families"—persons bound together by love and identity but not by name or bloodline. This is quite common in gay communities today as it was several generations ago. Forming families or small communities based on rejection by the larger community can also be a double-edged sword. While these can be positive, they may also turn into prisons of conformity. Does being lesbian, for example, mean everyone has short hair, hates men, and drives (or rides on) a motorcycle? *What Does It Mean to Be Gay, Lesbian, Bisexual, or Transgender?* "smashes" these and other stereotypes.

Another common misconception is that "all gay people are alike"—a classic example of a stereotypical statement. We may be drawn together because of a common prejudice or oppression, but we should not forfeit our individuality for the sake of the safety of a common identity, which is one of the challenges shown in *Gay People of Color: Facing Prejudices, Forging Identities*.

Coming out to who *you* are is just as important as having a group or "family" within which to safely come out. Becoming knowledgeable about these issues (through the books in this series and the other resources to which they will lead), feeling good about yourself, behaving safely, actively listening to others *and* to your inner spirit—all this will allow you to fulfill your promise and potential.

James T. Sears, PhD
Consultant

chapter 1

Mind, Body, and Spirit

Kara Blake is a healthy, vibrant, and proud woman. She's passionate about fighting for rights in the gay community, and she's always eager to get involved and assist young people through the complicated process of coming out.

But that wasn't always the case.

"If you'd known me a few years ago, you wouldn't believe it was the same person," she said. "Pretty much anything there was to do to ruin my body, I did it. And I did it a lot. I could say it was because I was unhappy about being gay, but it wasn't that simple. I thought I was unhappy being gay, but really I was just sad because I couldn't be me, the real me. And that kind of sadness hits you everywhere, inside and out."

When she was coming out in high school, Kara faced struggles that many young gay people experience. To help make herself feel better, or just to numb the pain, she began using drugs with her friends.

Feelings of shame and self-loathing are common in the young gay community, especially when faced with rejection from friends, family, schools, churches, and other influential people in their lives. Gay teens are at a significantly higher risk for mental health issues like depression, and these in turn can lead to substance abuse and even suicide.

"They face *discrimination*, *oppression*, and low self-esteem," said Julie A. Bock, director of an *LGBT* youth center in Wisconsin. "They also take more risks."

EXTRA INFO

Gay youth are four times more likely to attempt suicide than their heterosexual peers.

Bock's organization helped a young man named Darien Winston, who had left home when he was eighteen. After realizing he was gay four years earlier, he tried to kill himself twice. He believed he was doomed to go to hell because he was gay.

"There's so much in the world that's so painful—this shouldn't be one of them," said country singer Chely Wright, who came out in 2010. "This shouldn't be a reason a kid goes into his basement and puts a gun in his mouth. This shouldn't be a reason a

Country singer Chely Wright has spoken out on behalf of gays who are facing suicidal thoughts.

forty-five-year-old man takes a bottle of pills, but he does."

Of course, not all LGBT people take such a severe measure when they deal with the challenges of understanding their **sexual orientation**. But many other health issues also impact gay people differently from their heterosexual **peers**.

Even something as simple as going for a medical check-up can be frightening for LGBT people, so they are less likely to maintain this crucial aspect of a healthy

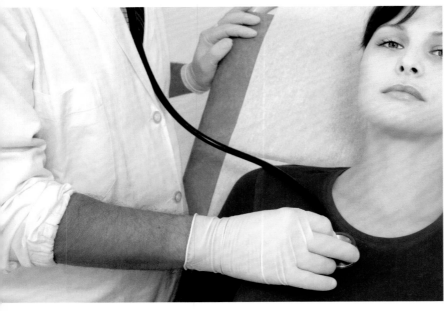

For a gay teen, going to the doctor for a routine checkup can seem like a frightening invasion of privacy.

Gay teens face many challenges to their self-esteem. If something as basic as your sexual identity is not accepted by your family, friends, and community, it can be very hard to feel good about yourself.

lifestyle. Many fear coming out to their doctors in case they face judgment or **prejudice** from physicians who don't typically treat gay patients.

"My mom always took me to the doctor when I was in school," said Kara. "So she would be sitting right there, and the doctor would ask me questions about sexual activities and things like that. Did I use drugs? What was I supposed to say? I couldn't tell the truth, because my mom would have gone crazy. So I lied."

She found herself lying about many things when faced with issues related to her sexual orientation. She couldn't be honest about who she was to her family or her friends, so being gay started to feel like a shameful secret. She began to hate herself for being gay.

That feeling is known as **internalized homophobia**. It occurs when external pressures—such as what comes from friends, family, or just society in general—send such strong homophobic messages that LGBT people believe there is something wrong with them.

What's That Mean?

Prejudice is an unfavorable opinion of a person or a group of people not based on actual knowledge.

When a person believes the prejudices other people have against them, those feelings are said to have become *internalized*.

Homophobia is the fear and hatred of homosexuality.

"I wished, each and every day, that I wasn't gay," said Kara. "If there was a pill that could have made me straight, I would have taken it, without a doubt. I wanted to just be normal. That's why I don't understand people who think being gay is a choice. I would never have chosen to feel that way. Never."

Those negative emotions and feelings of self-hatred took a physical toll on Kara. For years, she struggled with an eating disorder, abused drugs and alcohol, and engaged in risky sexual behavior that could have had severe consequences.

It wasn't until she found a supportive and welcoming group of friends in the LGBT community that she began to accept and love herself. Those feelings of anger and self-hatred no longer exist for her.

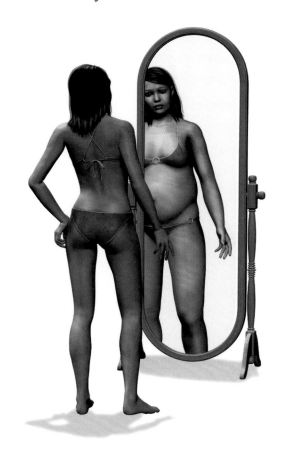

Gay teens are more likely to have eating disorders that cause them to view their bodies so critically that they perceive themselves to be ugly and overweight, even though they may in reality be thin (even dangerously so).

"Now I'd say, 'A straight pill? No thanks!'" she said with a smile. "I love who I am. I love my life. I wouldn't want to change any of it."

"Taking care of yourself and respecting yourself make all the difference. I didn't respect myself enough to stand up for myself. I let other people dictate to me how I was supposed to be and act. I let them beat me up, and I didn't even raise a hand to defend myself. So now, I just try to help kids see that it really does get better. It's not always going to be like that. But they have to care enough about themselves to take care of their minds and bodies."

Today, more than ever before, **advocacy** organizations exist to help LGBT people find the resources and support they need. At community centers like the one Bock leads, staff is trained to deal with even the most complicated and seemingly hopeless situations. They also can help young people deal with day-to-day challenges and questions.

"We work closely with young people to resolve whatever is going on in their lives. There is nothing that's forbidden," Bock said. "You want to talk about safe sex, that's fine. We go there. Whatever the crisis is, we help them resolve it."

LGBT centers offer discussion groups, social events,

What's That Mean?

Advocacy is the work of supporting something you believe in.

and classes on health and fitness. Most places provide condoms and information about safe sex. Some also offer rapid HIV testing that provides results in 20 minutes, making it easier for people to get accurate results quickly.

For those who don't have such centers in their area—or are afraid to visit them—there are hundreds

LGBT centers help teens accept their identities and form healthy relationships.

of resources online. The National Gay and Lesbian Task Force offers numerous resources for gay youth. The Trevor Project provides help for individuals considering suicide, including a 24-hour telephone help line. The GLBT National Help Center has peer-supported online chat, as well as toll-free peer-counseling support lines. The Gay and Lesbian Medical Association's website helps LGBT people find health care providers who are gay friendly and familiar with the specific needs of the gay community.

"It's so important to take care of yourself—your mind, body, and spirit," said Kara. "It's all connected. Someone can look perfect on the outside, but be a mess on the inside. And what good is that? That's never going to make you happy. You have to find your peace in life. That's what makes you feel good. When you are at peace with yourself and who you are, everything else just falls into place."

FIND OUT MORE ON THE INTERNET

Gay and Lesbian Medical Association
www.thebody.com/content/art13665.html

The National Gay and Lesbian Task Force
www.thetaskforce.org

The Trevor Project
www.thetrevorproject.org

READ MORE ABOUT IT

Hardin, Kimeron. *Loving Ourselves: The Gay and Lesbian Guide to Self-Esteem.* New York: Alyson Books, 2008.

Hardin, Kimeron N., Marny Hall, and Betty Berzon. *Queer Blues: The Lesbian and Gay Guide to Overcoming Depression.* Oakland, Calif.: New Harbinger, 2001.

chapter 2

Body Concept

Flipping through the pages of magazines, you'll see some pretty common images: beautiful skinny women, gorgeous men with fashionable clothes on perfectly-toned bodies, all revealing charming smiles and sparkling white teeth.

Men and Body Concept

Youth, beauty, and muscles—things gay men like Ed Wesley may enjoy looking at but don't necessarily relate to personally.

"We don't really have gay role models who are just ordinary-looking guys," he said. "It's all six-pack abs and beautiful young faces. The first 'big guy' gay man I've ever seen is on *Modern Family*."

He was referring to the television comedy centered on the changes in the traditional family. The show, which premiered in 2009, features gay couple Mitchell and Cameron. Mitchell is slender, but Cameron is bigger and bulkier—just like Ed.

But when Ed was first venturing out of the closet, decades before *Modern Family*, he recognized he didn't fit the traditional image of a gay man, making him feel like more of an outsider. To fit into the community, he felt pressure to conform to an image. After he came out, gay bars and clubs in West Hollywood were where he could go to meet people, but his large husky frame, pale skin, and bald head didn't fit the standard of sun-tanned men with chiseled muscles.

Although Ed learned to be comfortable with himself and his body, some gay men don't. About 20 percent of men with eating disorders are gay, according to psychotherapist Abigail H. Natenshon. Studies show this may be a reaction to something called "minority stress." This is the perceived need to meet mainstream standards of masculinity. For LGBT people, it can be combined with the fear of prejudice and even violence from others because they are gay. When threatened by homophobic people, some gay men feel they will be safer if they look like typical straight men.

"A lot of gay men who were sort of sissy boys . . . at school and were **effeminate** did feel themselves **emasculated**," said David, author of

What's That Mean?

A male who acts in a way that is considered to be "female" is said to be *effeminate*. It is usually used as an insult or "put down."

If a person feels *emasculated*, he feels as though his masculinity—his manhood—has been taken away from him.

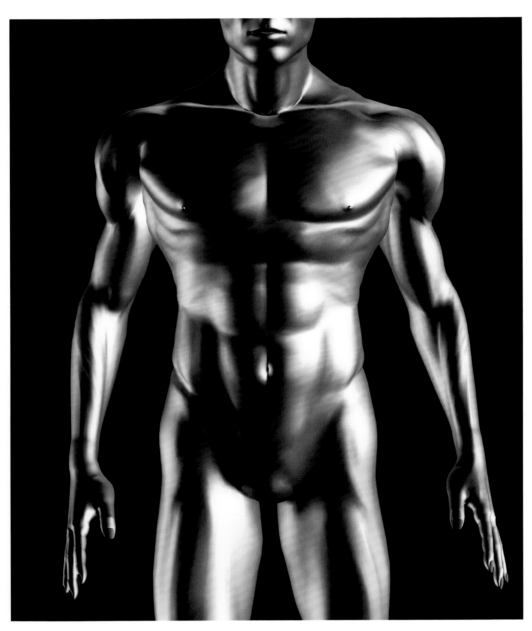

Stereotypical images of male masculinity can be difficult for young gay guys to live up to.

the novel *Fat Land: Thin Is In. Insides Are Out*. "So trying to attain a **definitive** male body is trying to regain some of that maleness for themselves. It's trying to reclaim their masculinity because they lost it so early on. And they kind of want it back, so they go for that male ideal of the big muscles and the six-pack and the strong chest and the flat stomach."

David is one of seven gay men who participated in *Do I Look Fat?*, a 2005 documentary about eating disorders and body image in the gay community. The film explores the "self-esteem disorder" in the gay community. It identifies a lack of support for young people coming out in high school that often leads to feelings of sadness, depression, and loneliness.

Stu, another subject of the film, recalled the effect his childhood had on his relationship with food. When he was in junior high school, he felt isolated and alone. "I remember being called a 'fag' even though I didn't know what it was," he said. "I remember walking to and from school. Most kids took the school bus, and I think, because I wanted to be by myself, I walked. And I remember stopping at the bakery and getting a chocolate éclair. Even then, I remember food was my friend, and it was very comforting to me."

David also sees many body image issues taking root in youth, when gay people are struggling to identify themselves, both in terms of sexual orientation as well as how they fit in with their peers.

"Guys who had extra weight on, guys who were walking around with a few more pounds, guys who had breasts or bellies—this was a female thing to have, a fuller figure," he said. "I was inactive and boys at school were always playing sports and always

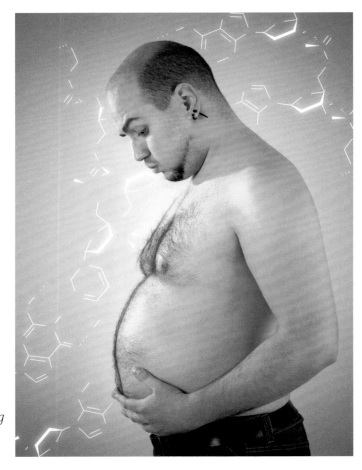

If a gay guy is a little chubby, he may feel as though he's not as masculine. Being gay does NOT mean being effeminate!

running around. So you do, in some ways, get emasculated as a fat kid. You don't necessarily really connect as a boy or a man."

That sense of not being a "real man" is even more complicated for young gay men, who have societal and cultural pressures telling them that being gay is weird or strange. And when this pressure becomes too intense, it can have damaging results.

"It's this [idea that] fat equals weak, equals female. Thin equals strong, equals male," David said. "And when you're gay, gay equals weak, equals female. So you do anything to be gay equals strong, equals man. And that means exercising to the point of extreme . . . or just not eating, full stop. Anything to be thin. Anything to be a man."

Some gay teens may feel as though the only way to have a male identity is to have a muscular physique.

EXTRA INFO

Eating disorders are psychiatric disorders characterized by abnormal eating habits that may involve either eating too much or too little, to the point that the level of food intake is dangerous to the individual's physical and emotional health. Binge eating disorder, bulimia nervosa, and anorexia nervosa are the most common eating disorders in the United States. The causes of eating disorders are complex and poorly understood, though it is clear they are often associated with other conditions and social situations; for example, one study found that girls with ADHD are many times more likely to develop certain eating disorders, and another found that women raised in foster care are also many times more likely to develop bulimia nervosa. It is generally thought that peer pressure and idealized body-types seen in the media are also a significant factor.

In the United States, 5 to 10 million women and about 1 million men have an eating disorder. While proper treatment can be effective for many of the specific types of eating disorder, the consequences of eating disorders can be severe, including death.

For some gay men, this can mean using steroids to enhance their muscles, working out at the gym obsessively, using drugs to lose weight and be thin, or developing an eating disorder. Each of these methods can have serious side effects that cause severe and lasting damage. Steroid use can cause high

Gay males may be tempted to use steroids to create the "manly" body they want for themselves.

Stereotypes **are the ways we expect a person or a group of people to act based on, for example, their race or sexual orientation. Stereotypes are often a form of prejudice.**

A *subculture* **is a smaller group of people with similar interests and lifestyles within a larger group.**

blood pressure and stunted growth in adolescents. Excessive exercise can cause damage to joints and ligaments, and the compulsive behavior often leads to eating disorders, which can cause malnutrition, dehydration, and muscle and tissue damage.

Women and Body Concept

Though women in the LGBT community can also struggle with body image and self-esteem, the issues are slightly different. Women in general, gay or straight, face pressure to fit into cultural *stereotypes* of how a female should appear. Supermodels with perfectly proportioned bodies are a difficult standard to live up to!

But studies have found that gay women are also influenced by a lesbian *subculture*, which in many ways rejects traditional roles for women. Lesbian teens trying to sort through their personal identity can then become very confused and conflicted about what they are expected to look like and be.

"When I was in high school, there were gay girls who were really athletic and on the soccer team or the softball team, and that wasn't me," said Kara Blake, who first recognized she was gay while in middle school. "I was a cheerleader. I didn't want to be butch or look like a boy. And because I wasn't, I didn't fit in with the people who were gay. So I tried even harder to fit in with my friends, but it was so difficult because I knew I wasn't like them. They wanted to look sexy and have boyfriends, and I just didn't. It was exhausting to try to live up to that."

Throughout high school, Kara battled depression, and eventually turned to drugs and alcohol to make her feel better about herself. She was so unhappy that she also began overeating and gained an unhealthy

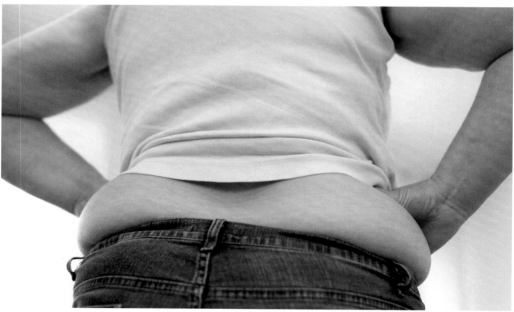

For a lesbian teenager, gaining weight may be a way to protect herself, to put up a barrier between herself and heterosexual relationships.

amount of weight. Through binge eating and drinking alcohol, she added 30 pounds to her once lean and fit frame.

"Then I didn't fit in anywhere," she said. "I think I did it because I didn't want the boys to be interested in me. Because then if they didn't want me, it wasn't because I was gay. It was them. So I didn't have to tell my friends that I wasn't with a boy because I was a lesbian. It was just because I was fat."

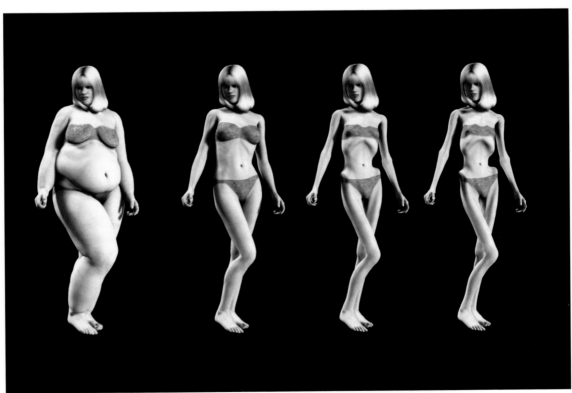

Gaining unhealthy amounts of weight, as well as losing unhealthy amounts of weight, can both be ways to avoid your own sexuality.

Jai, who was also featured in the documentary, had a similar perspective when he was struggling with his identity. He believed he could avoid issues of sexuality by making himself undesirable to other people.

Getting Help

"Part of the theory is that . . . if you're unsure of where you are, or if you're just not comfortable with where you're at, using the eating disorder is an incredibly effective way to feel nonsexual," he said. "And part of me probably knew this, making myself seem less appealing, looking sick, looking sad."

Jai was treated for his eating disorder and drug addiction. Part of the recovery process is about individuals establishing a healthy relationship with their bodies and themselves. Experts recommend that anyone struggling with body image issues or eating disorders should discuss the problem with a professional, a trusted friend, or in a support group. There are also rehabilitation centers to assist individuals with eating disorders, including Rogers Memorial Hospital in Wisconsin, which has a residential treatment facility specifically for men.

But the situation doesn't have to be quite so critical for people to take action. In fact, everyone benefits from being aware of their physical health and making sure they find a routine that works for them. In Ed's case, he tries to eat right and remain active.

He also has found social groups and activities where he is surrounded by people who look more like him. And he's never been happier.

Getting regular exercise and eating healthy foods are a necessity for all people, gay or straight. Simple exercises like walking or running provide opportunities to burn off calories—along with frustration and anger. Being in good physical condition helps improve an individual's overall body image and self-confidence. It increases self-esteem and personal satisfaction with life.

"I like looking good and feeling good, so that's why I go to the gym," said Jim Mansell, who is in a committed relationship and works out at least five times a week. "People think gay men go to the gym just to meet other guys or something. For some people, that's true. But it also makes you feel good about yourself. When I don't exercise or when I eat too much and just lay on the couch all day, I don't like the way I feel about myself. But when I exercise and keep myself healthy, I feel good about me. And that's most important to me."

FIND OUT MORE ON THE INTERNET

Homosexuals Are More Prone to Eating Disorders
news.softpedia.com/news/Homosexuals-Are-More-Prone-to-Eating-Disorders-51975.shtml

National Eating Disorders
www.nationaleatingdisorders.org

READ MORE ABOUT IT

Kaufman, Gershen and Lev Raphael. *Coming Out of Shame: Transforming Gay and Lesbian Lives*. Jackson, Tenn.: Main Street Books, 2006.

Kort, Joe. *Ten Smart Things Gay Men Can Do to Improve Their Lives*. New York: Alyson, 2003.

chapter 3

Self-Respect and Sexual Health

HIV/AIDS

If you ask someone to name a health issue affecting the gay community, you're probably going to get the same answer, over and over—AIDS, acquired immune deficiency syndrome.

Pride festivals are covered with posters promoting safe sex. Magazines advertise the latest drug treatment therapies. Mobile units park outside gay clubs to offer testing for HIV, human immunodeficiency virus, which causes AIDS.

"It's hard not to think of it as a gay disease," said Rob Kelly. "I don't know any straight people who have it. I mean, I know they do, but in my world, all I see or hear about is gay men. Practically every movie or TV show with gay characters has some mention of HIV. Straight people don't talk about it the way we do."

Like many other young people who didn't experience the AIDS *epidemic* and ensuing panic in the

1980s, he didn't consider HIV to be that much of a threat. People now live with HIV for decades without ever getting sick, and the illness isn't the death sentence it once was. So people aren't as cautious as they once were. That was true for Rob, who didn't rec-ognize the importance of regular testing and safe sex until he tested positive when he was twenty-one.

The AIDS/HIV epidemic is a dangerous and complicated reality. Not only does it put all teens at risk who engage in risky behaviors, but it also contributes to gay teens' feelings of shame and anxiety.

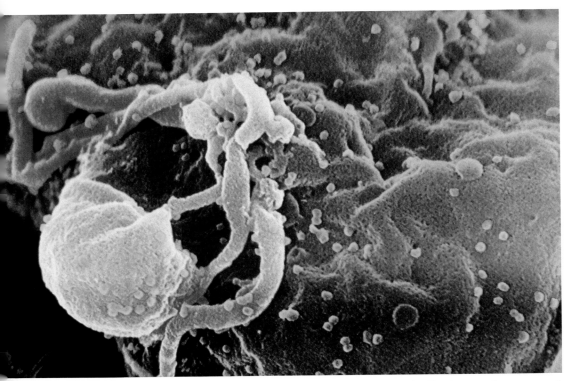

The HIV virus shown here is spread through body fluids—and anyone who engages in risky behaviors can catch it.

Worse, the virus had progressed so far in his system that it had already become AIDS by the time he even knew he was infected. This meant that the virus had attacked his system so severely that his T cells—the white blood cells that help the body fight infection—were almost gone.

The fact is that people who engage in risky sexual behaviors, no matter what their sexual orientation, are more at risk of contracting HIV. The disease has nothing to do with personal identity. It's about bodily fluids. Whenever bodily fluids are exchanged—whether through sexual intercourse between heterosexual partners, between same-sex partners, or through sharing needles for drugs—HIV can be transmitted.

The history of HIV and AIDS also closely mirrors the growth of the gay rights movement. When public action to stop the illness was slow to come in the 1980s, many attributed this to the fact that the disease was mostly appearing in the gay community. In fact, it was initially called GRID—gay-related immune deficiency. But the public slowly became aware of the universal nature of the illness when people outside the gay community became infected. Ryan White, a

EXTRA INFO

According to AVERT, an international AIDS charity based in the United Kingdom, 33 million people worldwide were living with HIV in 2008. Studies show that about two-thirds of infections were from heterosexual contact. Only about 10 percent had been passed along by men having sex with men.

In the United States, there were over a million cases of people living with HIV/AIDS in 2006. The following year, more than 42,000 new cases were reported by the thirty-three states with confidential reporting procedures in place, and the Centers for Disease Control and Prevention (CDC) estimates there were more than 56,000 nation-wide. About half of those are gay men.

EXTRA INFO

A sexually transmitted disease (STD), also known as sexually transmitted infection (STI) or venereal disease (VD), is an illness that is passed from person to person through sexual activity, including vaginal intercourse, oral sex, and anal sex. While in the past, these illnesses have mostly been referred to as STDs or VD, in recent years, the medical community has begun to prefer the term sexually transmitted infection (STI), since it has a broader range of meaning: a person may be infected, and may potentially infect others, without showing signs of disease. Some STIs can also be transmitted via the use of IV drug needles, as well as through childbirth or breastfeeding. Sexually transmitted infections have been well known for hundreds of years.

hemophiliac who was infected with HIV at thirteen from a blood transfusion, became nationally recognized when he was expelled from school because of his illness in 1984.

While HIV is an undeniable threat to gay men, it's also a significant risk for anyone who engages in sex without a condom, gay or straight. In 2004, 4,883 American youth between the ages of thirteen

What's That Mean?

A *hemophiliac* is someone who has a blood disease in which bleeding is uncontrolled.

and twenty-four were infected with HIV, and 232 young people with AIDS died.

Unsafe Sex

A CDC study showed that 47 percent of high school students are sexually active, often before they receive proper education on sexually transmitted diseases such as HIV, Chlamydia, herpes, and gonorrhea. Many don't realize that using condoms is one of the most effective ways of preventing transmission of these diseases.

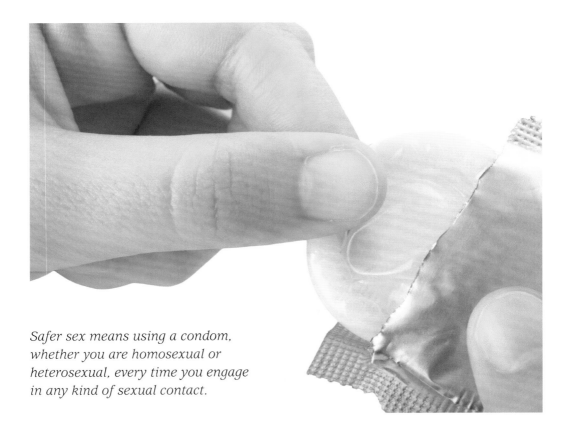

Safer sex means using a condom, whether you are homosexual or heterosexual, every time you engage in any kind of sexual contact.

"It is a very *taboo* subject among parents, teachers, everybody. We're hoping by opening up a more honest discussion that teenagers will reduce their amount of sexual activity or use contraception," said Julia Bair, a public health educator. "This is an issue that is so huge but it tends to get swept under the carpet because people don't want to talk about it."

It's not easy to talk about sex in general. And gay teens that aren't able to discuss their homosexuality with their parents are even more unlikely to take the measures necessary to protect themselves from sexually transmitted diseases. The CDC encourages all teens to protect themselves by using condoms, as well as having limited sexual partners or not engaging in sexual activity. Teenagers who are sexually active, need to be open and honest with their doctors, so they can be tested for possible infections and receive important information about sexual health.

"Discussions around sexual health are never easy or comfortable," said Dr. Marybeth McCall, chief medical officer for Excellus BlueCross BlueShield. "Until we start increasing awareness around the importance of regular screenings for at-risk individuals, many undiagnosed infected individuals will put their

What's That Mean?

Something that's *taboo* is forbidden.

Pregnancy brings with it an entire new set of responsibilities and health issues, and yet lesbian teens may prefer these challenges to revealing their sexual orientation.

health at risk by going untreated and will threaten the health of others by unknowingly spreading their infection."

The other primary risk of unprotected sex is pregnancy. In 2006, 750,000 teenagers in the United States became pregnant. Surprisingly, a significant

Lesbian teens may engage in heterosexual relationships as a way to conceal their true identities.

portion of these may be girls who identify as lesbian or bisexual. That was the finding of a study done in Canada, where 7.3 percent of lesbian teens and 10.6 percent of bisexual girls reported pregnancy.

While this may sound confusing, the reason is not difficult to understand. Many gay teens said they engaged in heterosexual sex so their classmates wouldn't suspect

What's That Mean?

Harassment is bullying, threats of violence, and other negative behaviors directed toward another person.

Discrimination is unfair treatment of people based on prejudice.

Stigma is a mark of shame.

they were gay. Similarly, the study found that a high percentage of gay and bisexual teen males were also involved with pregnancies.

"Those who experience **harassment** and **discrimination** may choose pregnancy involvement as a way to deny their orientation, to prevent further enacted **stigma**," the report stated.

As a high school student, Kara Blake was terrified her friends and family would find out she was gay. So to hide it, she had sex with several different boys. She hoped that if she did it enough, she might be able to force herself to be straight.

But she didn't have any romantic feelings for them, and she knew they didn't care about her. Each time, the encounters made her feel worse about herself, which made her increasingly depressed.

"It was so degrading, and it made me feel cheap and used," she said. "After a while, I didn't even care what happened anymore. I never got pregnant, but I could have, because I wasn't always safe. It didn't feel real to me, so I didn't think it mattered if I used a condom. But a lot of things could have happened to me because of that."

Do It for Yourself!

Safe sex may seem like a set of needless rules created by adults to control adolescents. But the reality is this: Safe sex isn't something you do for your parents. It's not something you do for your church or religious leader. You don't do it to please your teachers or your counselors. You do it for yourself.

Sexual health and self-respect go hand-in-hand. All the education, knowledge, and awareness in the world won't mean anything if people don't respect themselves enough to take precautions that will protect them. And this includes selecting appropriate sexual partners.

"To keep your body safe, you have to have pride, no matter if you're gay or straight," said Rob Kelly. "It's the pride of knowing that you're worth taking care of and you're worth protecting. It's not about what other people want or what they say or what they do.

It's about you, because the choices you make in one moment can affect your life forever."

FIND OUT MORE ON THE INTERNET

Avert
www.avert.org

Centers for Disease Control and Prevention
www.cdc.gov

READ MORE ABOUT IT

Vitkus, Jessica. *Safe Sex: Honest Expert Information to Answer All Your Questions*. New York: MTV, 2007.

Wolfe, Daniel. *Men Like Us: The GMHC Complete Guide to Gay Men's Sexual, Physical, and Emotional Well-Being*. New York: Ballantine, 2000.

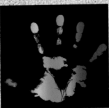

chapter 4

Substance Abuse

When Simon Fanshawe first came out, he was active in political movements to gain equal rights for gay people. His pride in himself and his community was evident in his lifestyle and attitude. So it surprised some people when he produced a documentary titled *The Trouble with Gay Men*.

"We've fought discrimination and prejudice, only to wreck ourselves with drugs," he said.

The film explores frightening trends of substance abuse within the gay community, highlighting an issue that *activists* around the world have been working tirelessly to resolve. Studies show that LGBT people are more likely to abuse drugs, alcohol, and tobacco than the general population.

The National Association of Lesbian and Gay Addition Professionals notes that LGBT

What's That Mean?

Activists are people who are involved in political or social movements.

people use drugs and alcohol for many of the same reasons other people do—as a way of coping with stress, depression, or pressure. But these factors are heightened in the gay community, where people often face homophobia and rejection by family and friends.

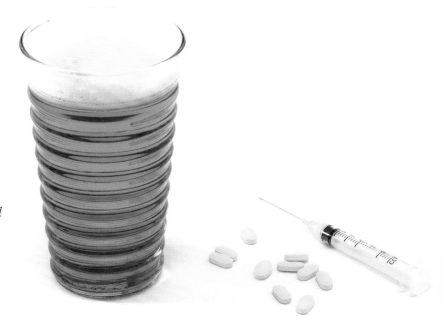

Gay teens often turn to drugs and alcohol to numb the pain they feel in the face of rejection and harassment.

These tensions can be especially difficult for young people. A 1995 study identified substance-abuse risk factors among teens and adolescents, including:

- feelings of being worthless or "bad"
- no support from peers and adults
- pressure to fit in
- no access to role models
- few opportunities to socialize with LGBT people outside of bars
- fear of contracting HIV

No wonder that substance abuse is so common among gay people!

Gays and Crystal Meth

Crystal methamphetamine, usually known as simply "crystal meth," became prevalent in the gay community as a drug used at parties because it would lower *inhibitions* and put people at ease.

What's That Mean?

Inhibitions are feelings of guilt and shame that keep us from doing things we might otherwise want to do.

Matt began using crystal meth when he was sixteen. At the time, he knew he was gay. He had tried to tell his parents in the past, but they made it clear that he would not be welcome at home if he lived what they called a "gay lifestyle." In his small town,

Crystal meth lowers inhibitions, making gays more comfortable with their attraction to the same sex.

his religious neighbors were openly homophobic, blaming gay people for drugs and AIDS.

"Whenever there would be stories in the paper or on the news about gay people, it always had something to do with drugs," he said. "My parents would just shake their heads and say, 'It figures.'"

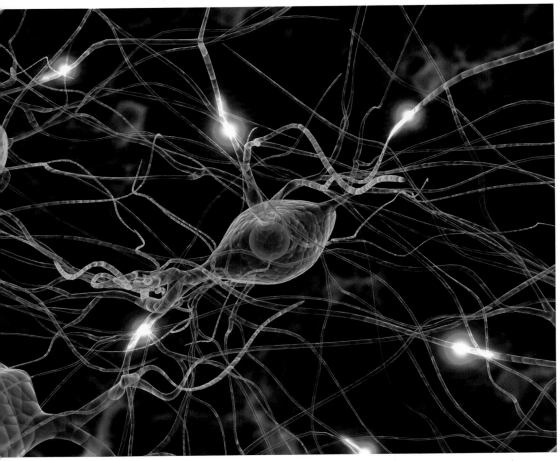

Meth can change the way the cells within your brain (your neurons) function.

He didn't find support at his school, either. He watched as an older male student came out and caused a panic in the school. Other students bullied him relentlessly, and parents wouldn't allow their sons to be in his gym class. A teacher even told Matt that the other student would get AIDS and die because he was gay.

"They were the people you trust, so I believed them," Matt said. "It didn't even occur to me to doubt them, or to think that maybe they didn't know what they were talking about. I knew I would never, ever tell. I couldn't. I just wanted to get out of there."

He began sneaking out of the house and going to gay bars and clubs. Ashamed of what he was doing and what it could mean for him, he began using crystal meth and other club drugs.

"It made me feel like nothing mattered," he said. "I didn't have to care about anything. I wasn't scared of anything. I was just so out of it, anything could have happened to me."

Crystal meth forces the brain to produce chemicals that create feelings of pleasure. While this doesn't sound like a bad thing, the drug causes these chemicals to be released extremely quickly, which leads to the rush of good feelings. Using crystal meth actually changes how the brain functions, and some of these changes continue after the drug use stops. Long-term users of crystal meth are often unable to

Gay teens who have been rejected by their families may end up living on the streets.

produce these chemicals naturally, and so become completely addicted to the drug. Crystal meth also significantly impairs brain function during use.

Drugs and Risky Behaviors

While using crystal meth, Matt had unprotected sex with people he didn't know. That type of behavior is common among crystal meth users, which has led to an increase in HIV infection rates. It's one of the many severe consequences of the drug that also causes mental health issues, brain damage, and even death.

Matt's drug abuse became so bad that he barely graduated high school. Then one night he came home drunk and stoned after a night out. He got into an argument with his parents and blurted out his secret—that he was gay. They immediately told him to leave. For the next year, he spiraled out of control and even lived on the street for a period of time.

"I continued that way for so long, I don't know how I'm still alive," said Matt, who also used cocaine, marijuana, and abused prescription medications. "I should be dead now. And the whole time, I thought it was because I was gay. It was my punishment. That's what they always told me. If you're gay, you're going to use drugs and your life will be ruined. And when that's what happened, I thought they were right."

Sitting in a bar one night, barely conscious, Matt was "probably a few steps away from being dead."

Self-hatred can lead to dangerous behaviors, creating a destructive vicious circle.

He was living with a much older man because he had no place else to go. The man he lived with would buy him food and drugs in exchange for sex.

"I felt like my life was worthless, so I didn't care what happened to it," he said. "It was all just about getting more drugs. It didn't matter what I had to do."

Then he met a social worker from a local LGBT community center. She told him about some of the support groups and programs the center offered, and invited him to visit. He did, and it changed his life.

"She saved my life," Matt said. "She helped me get clean. Now I'm in college. I have a boyfriend and a job. I'm really happy. And I'm proud of myself. I have respect for myself now, which I never had before.

"I didn't think I'd be able to have this, because I'm gay. And I think a lot of other people think that, too. That's why there's so much drugs and drinking. People don't know it's okay, that they can have something better."

Lesbians and Alcohol Abuse

Among lesbians, excessive alcohol use is far more prevalent than among heterosexual women. Kara Blake, whose difficulty accepting herself as a lesbian led to overeating and drug abuse, began drinking alcohol when she went to gay bars to meet people.

"It was like that was the only option," she said. "That's what you did on Friday and Saturday nights.

You go to the bar. Then it became Sunday, Monday, Tuesday, every day. You'd meet people, but of course they would drink too much, too. So then the relationship would be unhealthy because it was based on something so unhealthy. It was just a crazy cycle that didn't really make any sense. But it's not like you could just go meet a girl at the grocery store and ask her out. At least at a gay bar, you know everyone is gay."

Once Kara got involved in an organization for gay students at her college, she began to meet new people and found activities that didn't involve drugs or alcohol. She also participated in campaigns to help

Lesbians are more apt to abuse alcohol than straight women, often in an attempt to cope with their feelings of loneliness and pain.

Smoking can be a form of self-destructive behavior, one that lesbians are more likely to do than are heterosexual women.

teach other people about the dangers of substance abuse.

"I don't think people really understand just how dangerous it is, because it just looks like fun," she said. "But if you look at the statistics, the number of gay people who get into serious trouble, you really see that this is something that is destroying our community."

Tobacco Use

Instances of tobacco use among gay adults, especially lesbians, are almost twice as high among the overall adult population. Smoking is one of the leading factors that contribute to poor health among LGBT people, and gay teens are four times more likely to smoke than their straight peers.

"Smoking is one of things that you see so much in bars, you forget that it's even a negative," said Kara. "Everyone smokes at gay bars. Even people who don't smoke other places. It's about fitting in."

Finding Options

When people feel they don't belong any place else, they sometimes do what they think they must do to fit in. That was the case for Kara and Matt, both of whom participated in 12-step recovery programs to overcome their addictions.

Increased use of drugs and alcohol is also common among individuals who are HIV positive, particularly

When you like yourself, when you have friends who accept you the way you are, you don't need to abuse drugs or engage in other risky behaviors.

gay men. One of the reasons for this is likely the hopelessness some people feel at having an illness that cannot be cured.

Stu, an avid activist for gay health issues in San Francisco, began using drugs and alcohol when he was a teenager. Influenced by his parents, also heavy drinkers, he used drugs and alcohol as a way to escape his feelings of low self-esteem that resulted from being an overweight kid.

"I tested HIV positive in the late 1980s and felt that I now had permission to drink and do drugs without restriction. I wallowed in self pity," said Stu, who was also a subject of the 2005 documentary *Do I Look Fat?*

Eventually, he got clean and focused on improving his overall health. He has lived with his illness for decades, and he now sees that it is not an excuse for allowing himself to fall victim to drugs and alcohol.

Many resources exist for individuals with substance-abuse issues. In many communities, LGBT organizations offer Alcoholics Anonymous and Narcotics Anonymous meetings specifically for gay people. And rehabilitation treatment centers can be found across the country.

EXTRA INFO

Twelve-step recovery programs are based on the successful methods used by Alcoholics Anonymous. People in these programs pass through twelve stages, or steps, toward addiction recovery.

The most important thing is education and awareness. Numerous organizations have developed public education campaigns to make people more aware of the dangers of drug and alcohol abuse. Studies have shown that such campaigns have reduced use of crystal meth in the gay community. And peer-based outreach has been even more successful. Within the gay community, activists have begun to focus on using the pride in the community's history to help reduce the shame associated with homosexuality.

"Once I started seeing being gay as just a part of who I am, and I accepted and loved that, I was so much happier," Matt said. "I didn't need drugs, and I didn't need to get drunk. I was happy with myself."

FIND OUT MORE ON THE INTERNET

Gay-Friendly Rehab
www.gay-rehab.com

Gay, Lesbian, Bisexual and Substance Abuse
www.mcgill.ca/studenthealth/information/queerhealth/glbsub-stanceabuse

READ MORE ABOUT IT

Kominars, Kathryn. *Accepting Ourselves and Others: A Journey into Recovery.* Center City, Minn.: Hazelden, 2006.

Osborne, Duncan. *Suicide Tuesday: Gay Men and the Crystal Meth Scare.* Cambridge, Mass.: Da Capo, 2005.

Sanello, Frank. *Tweekers: How Crystal Meth Is Ravaging Gay America.* New York: Alyson, 2005.

BIBLIOGRAPHY

Crawford, Tiffany. "Pregnancy Risk Rises for Teens in the Closet." *Ottawa Citizen*, April 28, 2010.

Doyle, Ieva. "Sexually Transmitted Diseases: The Silent Epidemic." *The Ithaca Journal,* April 27, 2010.

Johnson, Ramon. "Gay Men and Eating Disorders." About.com.

Kelly, Laura. "Lesbian Body Image Perceptions." *Qualitative Health Research,* 2007.

Kimmel, Sara B. and Mahalik, James R. "Body Image Concerns of Gay Men: The Roles of Minority Stress and Conformity to Masculine Norms." *Journal of Consulting and Clinical Psychology,* December 2005.

"Lesbian Body Image Differs from That of Women Overall." *The Medical News*, March 15, 2005.

Ocamb, Karen. "Country Star Chely Wright Comes Out, Talks About Suicide, God, Melissa, kd and the Indigo Girls." *The Huffington Post,* May 6, 2010.

"The Real Costs of Teen Pregnancy," Washington D.C. National Campaign to Prevent Teen Pregnancy, September 2006.

Rowe, Aaron. "Meth Use Among Gay Men Decreasing; Other Drug Use Holding Steady." *Wired*, July 26, 2007.

Salyer, David. "Getting It Straight: HIV as a Gay Disease Is a Myth That Refuses to Die." *The Body*, March 1999.

Sloth, Paul. "Survey: Teens Uninformed About Sex." *The Journal Times,* May 7, 2010.

Thomas-Lynn, Felicia. "LGBT Center Helps Gay Teens at Risk." *Journal Sentinel*, May 8, 2010.

White, Hilary. "Homosexual U.K. Documentarian Says Gay Lifestyle a 'Sewer' of Casual Degrading Sex, Drug Abuse and Misery." LifeSiteNews, September 10, 2008.

INDEX

ABOUT THE AUTHOR AND THE CONSULTANT

Jaime A. Seba's involvement in LGBT issues began in 2004, when she helped open the doors of the Pride Center of Western New York, which served a community of more than 100,000 people. As head of public education and outreach, she spearheaded one of the East Coast's first crystal methamphetamine awareness and harm reduction campaigns. She also wrote and developed successful grant programs through the Susan G. Komen Breast Cancer Foundation, securing funding for the region's first breast cancer prevention program designed specifically for gay, bisexual, and transgender women. Jaime studied political science at Syracuse University before switching her focus to communications with a journalism internship at the Press & Sun-Bulletin in Binghamton, New York, in 1999. She is currently a freelance writer based in Seattle.

James T. Sears specializes in research in lesbian, gay, bisexual, and transgender issues in education, curriculum studies, and queer history. His scholarship has appeared in a variety of peer-reviewed journals and he is the author or editor of twenty books and is the Editor of the Journal of LGBT Youth. Dr. Sears has taught curriculum, research, and LGBT-themed courses in the departments of education, sociology, women's studies, and the honors college at several universities, including: Trinity University, Indiana University, Harvard University, Penn State University, the College of Charleston, and the University of South Carolina. He has also been a Research Fellow at Center for Feminist Studies at the University of Southern California, a Fulbright Senior Research Southeast Asia Scholar on sexuality and culture, a Research Fellow at the University of Queensland, a consultant for the J. Paul Getty Center for Education and the Arts, and a Visiting Research Lecturer in Brazil. He lectures throughout the world.